MW01101231

DOGS THROUGHOUT HISTORY™

The Story of the Saint Bernard

Jennifer Quasha

The Rosen Publishing Group's
PowerKids Press™
New York

For Scout

Published in 2000 by The Rosen Publishing Group, Inc.
29 East 21st Street, New York, NY 10010

First Edition

Book design: Danielle Primiceri

Photo credits: Cover © Adamsmith 1995/FPG International; pp. 4, 11 © Archive Photos; p. 7 © Ralph Reinhold/Animals Animals; p. 8 © Anton Kamp © Archive Photos; p. 12 © Frank Roche/Animals Animals; p. 15 Courtesy of the Natural History Museum of Switzerland; p. 16 © Richard Kolar/Animals Animals; p. 19 © SuperStock; p. 20 © Everett Collection.

Quasha, Jennifer
      The story of the Saint Bernard / by Jennifer Quasha.
          p.   cm.— (Dogs throughout history)
      Includes index.
      Summary: Discusses the physical characteristics, history, and uses of the Saint Bernard, known for its rescue work.
      ISBN 0-8239-5517-6 (lib. bdg.)
      1. Saint Bernard dog—History—Juvenile literature. 2. Saint Bernard dog—Juvenile literature. [1. Saint Bernard dog. 2. Dogs.] I. Title. II. Series.
      SF429.S3Q37   1999
      636.73—dc21   98-49450
                                                                                           CIP
                                                                                           AC

Manufactured in the United States of America

Contents

All About the Saint Bernard

The Saint Bernard is a great big dog that can weigh up to 200 pounds. That's more than some very tall grown-ups weigh. The dog's base **coat** color is white with red, brown, or black markings. Saint Bernards usually live around eight to ten years. They are called working dogs because they have been helping humans over one thousand years. In their long history, Saint Bernards have helped, loved, and lived with millions of people around the world.

◀ *Saint Bernards have thick, shaggy coats that need to be brushed.*

The Saint Bernard Is Born

The history of the Saint Bernard dates back a very long time. Many people believe that Saint Bernards were first born around 200 A.D. in the European country of Switzerland. The Saint Bernard may have been **bred** from an unknown type of dog **native** to Switzerland and another type of dog called a Molosser. The Molosser was an Asian dog that was brought to Switzerland by Roman armies. These dogs were **mated**, and the first Saint Bernard puppies were born.

Saint Bernards, like this one, have feathered tails. ▶

Saint Bernards at Work

The first Saint Bernards lived on farms **nestled** in the valleys of a large mountain range called the Swiss Alps. They were large dogs that helped the Swiss people with many jobs around their farms. They also guarded the farmers' homes and land by barking if a stranger approached. Some Saint Bernards helped the farmers **herd** their cows and sheep from one place to another. Others were used like horses. They were attached to wagons and carts. They were so strong they could pull carts from one place to another. This type of Saint Bernard was called a **talhund**, which means a valley dog, or **bauerhund**, which means a farm dog. The name depended on where the dog lived.

◀ *Saint Bernards are known to drool a lot!*

The Hospice in the Alps

Many years ago, in 1050 A.D., an archdeacon named Bernard de Menthon founded a hospital in the Swiss Alps. This hospital was called a **hospice** and was built in order to take care of travelers who got sick while they were hiking on dangerous trails between Italy and Switzerland. At this time there were no railroads or cars or buses to get from one place to another. People had to travel by foot. Religious men called **monks** lived in the hospice. Saint Bernard dogs were brought to the hospice to keep the monks company during the long, cold winter months. They were given their name after the founder of the hospice, Bernard de Menthon.

The monks from the hospice walk with a team of Saint Bernard rescue dogs. ▶

Saint Bernards to the Rescue

Around 1660, the monks at the hospice realized they could teach their smart dogs to help find lost travelers in the snow. The Saint Bernard has such a powerful sense of smell that it can smell a person buried under seven feet of snow. After finding the person, the Saint Bernard would dig him out of the snow. Then, he would lie down next to him, and use his body heat to warm the man. The dog would also lick the person's face to try to wake him up. People today believe that Saint Bernards saved over 2,000 men and women during their time at the hospice.

◀ *Saint Bernards can dig deep, through lots of snow.*

The Most Famous Saint Bernard

A Saint Bernard named Barry is probably the most famous Saint Bernard in history. Barry lived at the hospice in the Swiss Alps from 1800 to 1812. Many people say that Barry saved more than 40 travelers' lives! There is a **legend** that Barry was mistaken for a wolf and shot to death by the 41st person he tried to rescue. This story is not true. The real reason that this heroic dog died was from old age in 1814. Today, in Bern, Switzerland, there is a statue of Barry in the Natural History Museum.

Barry was a very brave and special Saint Bernard. ▶

Saint Bernards Around the World

Many years later, in the late 1850s, a Swiss man named Heinrich Schumacher wanted other Saint Bernards to be as smart and courageous as the famous Barry. Schumacher was a butcher and innkeeper, as well as a dog lover. He worked hard to make sure the Saint Bernard puppies he bred were born healthy and strong.

Heinrich Schumacher was also **responsible** for selling his Saint Bernards to people in other countries, as well as his native Switzerland. He sent Saint Bernards to places such as England, Russia, and the United States of America. Soon Saint Bernards became one of the most popular dogs throughout the world.

◄ *The upper and lower lips of the Saint Bernard are called flews.*

A Friendly Dog

Saint Bernards are big, friendly dogs that love to play with children. They are smart and easily trained. It is very important to train Saint Bernards when they are puppies because when they grow to their full size, training becomes much harder. Saint Bernards love to exercise, and they need time to run and play outdoors every day. They love to eat. Some owners buy their Saint Bernard's food in very large 100-pound bags.

This little puppy will grow very big and probably weigh around 200 pounds! ▶

A Saint Bernard Named Beethoven

In 1992, a movie called *Beethoven* was released. It starred a Saint Bernard. This movie introduced the large and lovable dog to millions of Americans. *Beethoven* was about a puppy named Beethoven who escaped from a pet store. He ran away from robbers who wanted to steal him. Fortunately, Beethoven found a happy home with the Newtons where he was cared for by the whole family. *Beethoven* was such a success that the following year, movie producers made a sequel, *Beethoven's 2nd*. After seeing these movies, many young Americans wanted an adorable Saint Bernard of their own.

◄ *Many families wanted a big, lovable Saint Bernard after seeing the movie* Beethoven's 2nd.

21

Saint Bernards Today

Throughout their long history, Saint Bernards have been considered heroes for many reasons. Saint Bernards have been helpful to people in work and play for many years. They still are today. These special dogs have helped farmers with their hard work. Saint Bernards have saved dying travelers. They have always given their owners love and affection. Saint Bernards have even starred in their own movies, which have made them one of the most popular dogs today.

Web Sites:

http://www.angelfire.com/ky/noblefriend/index.html
http://www.nbb.emory.edu/saint^

Glossary

bauerhund (BAH-wer-hoond) A German word for a farm dog.

bred (BREHD) A male and female animal that have been brought together so that they can have babies.

coat (COHT) An animal's fur.

herd (HURD) To watch over animals and keep them together in a group.

hospice (HAHS-pis) A place kept by monks where sick travelers may stay.

legend (LEH-jhund) A story that is passed down through the years and that many people believe.

mated (MAYT-id) A special joining of a male and female body. After mating, a baby may grow inside the female's body.

monks (MUNKS) Men who give up everything else for religion.

native (NAY-tiv) Coming from a certain area.

nestled (NEH-suld) Sheltered and protected.

responsible (reh-SPAHN-sih-bul) Being the cause or the reason for something.

talhund (TAHL-hoond) A German word for a dog from the valley.

23

Index